Cuban Americans

Hispanic Americans: Major Minority

Cuban Americans

Frank DePietro

Mason Crest

Mason Crest
370 Reed Road
Broomall, Pennsylvania 19008
www.masoncrest.com

Printed and bound in the United States of America.

First printing
9 8 7 6 5 4 3 2 1

Library of Congress Cataloging-in-Publication Data to come

DePietro, Frank.
Cuban Americans / by Frank DePietro.
    p. cm.
Includes index.
ISBN 978-1-4222-2318-5 (hardcover) — ISBN 978-1-4222-2315-4 (series hardcover) — ISBN 978-1-4222-9322-5 (ebook)
  1. Cuban Americans—Juvenile literature. 2. Cuban Americans—History—Juvenile literature. 3. Cuban Americans—Biography History—Juvenile literature. I. Title.
E184.C97D46 2013
973'.04687291—dc23
                          2012010418

Produced by Harding House Publishing Services, Inc.
www.hardinghousepages.com
Interior design by Micaela Sanna.
Cover design by Torque Advertising + Design.
Printed in USA.

Contents

Introduction

by José E. Limón, Ph.D.

Even before there was a United States, Hispanics were present in what would become this country. Beginning in the sixteenth century, Spanish explorers traversed North America, and their explorations encouraged settlement as early as the sixteenth century in what is now northern New Mexico and Florida, and as late as the mid-eighteenth century in what is now southern Texas and California.

Later, in the nineteenth century, following Spain's gradual withdrawal from the New World, Mexico in particular established its own distinctive presence in what is now the southwestern part of the United States, a presence reinforced in the first half of the twentieth century by substantial immigration from that country. At the close of the nineteenth century, the U.S. war with Spain brought Cuba and Puerto Rico into an interactive relationship with the United States, the latter in a special political and economic affiliation with the United States even as American power influenced the course of almost every other Latin American country.

The books in this series remind us of these historical origins, even as each explores the present reality of different Hispanic groups. Some of these books explore the contemporary social origins—what social scientists call the "push" factors—behind the accelerating Hispanic immigration to America: political instability, economic underdevelopment and crisis, environmental degradation, impoverished or wholly absent educational systems, and other circumstances contribute to many Latin Americans deciding they will be better off in the United States.

And, for the most part, they will be. The vast majority come to work and work very hard, in order to earn better wages than they would back home. They fill significant labor needs in the U.S. economy and contribute to the economy through lower consumer prices and sales taxes.

When they leave their home countries, many immigrants may initially fear that they are leaving behind vital and important aspects of their home cultures: the Spanish language, kinship ties, food, music, folklore, and the arts. But as these books also make clear, culture is a fluid thing, and these native cultures are not only brought to America, they are also replenished in the United States in fascinating and novel ways. These books further suggest to us that Hispanic groups enhance American culture as a whole.

Our country—especially the young, future leaders who will read these books—can only benefit by the fair and full knowledge these authors provide about the socio-historical origins and contemporary cultural manifestations of America's Hispanic heritage.

Each chapter features the work of Cuban artist Luis Rodríguez. His bright colors, whimsical style, and lively compositions represent the heart of Cuban culture.

chapter 1
It Takes All Sorts

What do you think a normal American is like? What does a normal American say? What does she look like? What kind of clothes does he wear? What music would she like? What kind of job would he have?

It's hard to answer those questions. It's pretty hard to describe a normal American. There are so many people in America. There isn't just one sort of person who is normal.

Americans look different from each other. They have different jobs. They wear different clothes. They listen to different kinds of music.

Lots of different people live in the United States. Millions, in fact. Cuban Americans are one sort of American. There are actually over a million Cuban Americans alone.

Culture and Diversity

Cuban Americans all share a culture. The word culture gets used a lot. But what is culture exactly? It's a hard idea to figure out.

Culture is a bunch of things that one group of people shares. Culture is made up of customs. It is made up of beliefs. It is made up of art. Music, food, and religion is all part of culture. It's the way people think about life and the world.

Culture is sort of like a glue. It binds people together. Cuban Americans share a culture. Americans as a whole share a culture too. So do people from Germany. Or people from Thailand.

If you're American, you share things in common with other Americans. You have the same government. You probably speak at least some English. You go to an American school.

But maybe you have another culture, too. If you're Cuban American, you also belong to that culture. You might eat Cuban food. You might speak Spanish. You might be Catholic, like a lot of Cubans. People can have more than one culture.

American culture hasn't stayed the same forever. Think about it. We don't still use horses and carriages to get around. Most people don't believe in the Puritan religion like the first Americans did. We listen to very different music than Americans used to.

Cultures change over time. They also mix together. If two cultures meet, then they change each other. They both learn new ideas and new ways of doing things.

America is a diverse country made up of many different cultures.

CUBAN AMERICANS

Sometimes, something entirely new is created. For example, slaves from West Africa brought their music to the United States. Over time, that music mixed with music that was already in the United States. In the end, the music changed. Jazz music is one kind of music that came out of that mixture.

It's pretty interesting when cultures mix. New, exciting things happen. The United States has a lot of that cultural mixing going on.

People from all over the world live in the United States. There are people from Africa. There are people from Europe. There are people from Latin America. Someone from just about every country in the world lives in the United States.

The United States has a lot of diversity. That means that there are people of all different kinds living here. There are people who have British ancestors. There are people who have Mexican ancestors. There are people with different religions. There are people who have different jobs. Some people speak different languages.

In the past, diversity has led to bad things. People don't always understand each other's cultures. So they didn't get along. Sometimes it got violent. People fought. They did horrible things to each other.

Children in the Cuban American community.

It Takes All Sorts

Today, things are getting better. But people still don't always appreciate diversity. Sometimes people are scared of other people who look or act different from themselves. They worry that those people are going to hurt them in some way.

But really, America's diversity is a good thing! All those different people have different ideas. They have different kinds of art. They have different food. All together, it makes life more interesting to have variety. Cuban Americans, like all the other cultures in the United States, add lots of good things to America.

A Melting Pot? Or a Mosaic?

A lot of people say the United States is a melting pot. There are lots of different cultures here. But once they meet in the United States, they all become one thing. They melt into each other. Everyone becomes an American.

Sometimes that's true. People who move to the United States start being like other Americans. They might start speaking English. Or eating American food. Or any number of other things.

But for some people, the United States isn't a melting pot at all. Some people, especially people who just moved to the United States, don't want to lose their culture. They like living in America. But they don't want to forget who they are.

A better way to think of the United States is as a mosaic. A mosaic is a picture made out of lots of tiles glued together. From far away, it looks like one big picture. But close up, you can see all the individual parts.

That's a lot like the United States. From far away, we're all one country. If you take a closer look, we're all individual people. Each person is slightly different. Some of them have different cultures. All those differences are what make the entire picture.

Each tile in a mosaic keeps its unique identity, just as cultural groups within the United States have their own characteristics and values.

Cuban restaurants give Cuban culture to the United States.

Americans from Cuba

Cuban Americans are some of those tiles that make up the mosaic. Many Cuban Americans have kept their culture from Cuba. They are still American. They also remember their roots in Cuba. They still have a Cuban culture.

There are lots of Cubans in America. Some have just **immigrated** to the United States. They were born in Cuba and moved to America.

Some are Cuban Americans. They might have been immigrants but they are now United States citizens. Others were born in the United States and are citizens. But someone in their family moved to the United States. It could have been their parents. Or their grandparents. Or even further back.

> **Immigrated** *means moved from one country to live in another.*

CUBAN AMERICANS

Many of the Cubans who immigrated to the United States meant to go back to Cuba. They didn't think they were moving to America permanently.

A lot of them were forced to leave Cuba. They were exiles. An exile is someone who is forced to leave his or her country. They will be arrested or punished if they don't leave.

Many Cubans are political exiles. This means they didn't agree with how the government in Cuba should be run. Then, the government forced them to leave. That has been happening for almost two hundred years in Cuba.

Luis Rodríguez, Camino a Cristo

16

chapter 2
An Island Home

Cuba has a long history. It helps explain who Cubans are. It also helps to explain why some Cubans ended up in the United States.

Cuba is an island to the south of the United States. It is in the Caribbean Sea. It's only ninety miles away from Florida.

The Old World

Everybody knows that Columbus came to the Americas in 1492. He was the first European to discover that a whole new world existed across the ocean. But people already lived in that "New World."

To them, it was the only world. They had lived there a long time. These people are called Natives. There were many different groups of Natives. The most famous were the Maya, the Inca, and the Aztec.

They all ruled over different parts of Latin America. Many Native groups were very smart. They built huge pyramids. They were **astronomers**. They created beautiful art.

> **Astronomers** *are people who study the stars.*

Native people lived all the way from the very north of North America to the very south of South America. They lived everywhere in between. There were also Native people who lived in what today we call Cuba.

The native people in Cuba were called the Arawak. Other groups of Arawak also lived in the rest of the islands in the Caribbean.

For a long time, all those Natives lived their own lives. But then these people's lives would change. Another group of people arrived—the Europeans.

Worlds Collide

Once Columbus set foot on the shores of the Americas, everything changed. Suddenly, the Natives had to deal with new people.

Columbus was an explorer for Spain. He took lots of men with him when he set sail. After a long time sailing, he landed in the Bahamas in the Caribbean.

The men explored a bunch of islands. They found some gold. They made people into slaves.

SICKNESS AND DISEASE

Lots of natives died after the Spanish came to the Caribbean. Some were killed by the Spanish with weapons. Most died because of germs. The Spanish brought germs with them from Europe. The people who lived in the Caribbean had never run into these germs before. Their bodies couldn't fight the germs.

The Spanish brought lots of sickness. They brought smallpox. They brought measles. They brought the flu. Today, we have vaccinations for all these diseases. (That's why you get shots—to keep you from getting these diseases.) We also have medicine and hospitals. Back then, no one had these things. If you got the flu, you could die.

Sometimes people were lucky. Their bodies could fight flu or measles germs. Lots of Spanish people could. None of the Natives could, though. Thousands and thousands of them died.

CUBAN AMERICANS

When Columbus went to Spain, he told everybody about what he had found. He told them about the gold and jewels. He told them about the Natives, who they could make in to slaves. He told them about how warm and beautiful it was.

No wonder more people wanted to go there! Soon, lots of Spaniards were sailing to the Caribbean.

There, they found the Arawak people. They could have become friends with them. Instead they treated them cruelly. Thousands of people suffered.

One hundred and fifty years later, almost all the Arawaks had disappeared. Some had been killed by the Spanish. Some had died from diseases that the Spanish brought with them. Others ran away to other parts of Latin America.

The landing of Columbus.

Spanish Cuba

Cuba was one of the islands that the Spanish took over. Explorers hoped to find gold there. They didn't actually find very much. Instead, they made money a different way. They did something horrible. They made the Arawaks into slaves and sold them.

Cuba was important to Spain for other reasons too. Cuba is very close to both Florida and Mexico. So it made trade easier between these two places. Ships could stop at Cuba for supplies on the way to somewhere else.

It also helped the Spanish explore other parts of the New World. They set up a base on Cuba. Then they could send out people to explore Florida.

Finally, Cuba had very good soil. It could grow a lot of food and other crops. The Natives had grown corn, potatoes, cotton, and tobacco. Europeans had never seen any of these things. But they liked them.

> **Plantations** *are like enormous farms. They usually grow just one crop. They need lots of workers.*

The Spanish took the land from the Arawaks. Then they planted it with all those crops. Then they sold the crops to make money and feed themselves.

They figured out that something else grew well in Cuba, too. That was sugarcane, from which sugar is made. The Spanish created huge **plantations** to grow sugarcane.

A Spanish person ran each plantation. They used slaves to grow the sugarcane. They used Native slaves. But they also used African slaves.

The Natives didn't take all of this lying down. When the Spanish first came, they rebelled. A man named Hatuey led the rebellion.

Hatuey came to Cuba one day, before the Spanish first arrived. He had just come from another island where the Spanish had killed everyone. He warned the Arawak people that white people were coming. He warned them that the white people killed Natives.

Hatuey wanted the Arawaks to hide in the mountains with him. Then they could attack the Spanish. But no one really listened to him. They stayed. Most of them were killed by the Spanish when they came.

But Hatuey and a few people in the mountains did fight back. It didn't work though. The Spanish had better weapons. And there weren't enough Native rebels. So Hatuey was captured and killed.

By the 1600s, the people of Cuba looked very different from the way they had before. Before, only Natives lived in Cuba. Now, no Natives lived

A picture of the Arawak drawn long ago.

21

A painting of Spain's Cuba.

there. They had all been killed or chased away. Instead, all sorts of people lived there. And not all of them were equal.

The most powerful people were the Spanish. They came directly from Spain. They were the richest people. They controlled the government. They owned the plantations. They were in the army.

Everybody else was less powerful. There were *criollos*. These were Spanish people who had been born in Cuba. Their families were Spanish. But they had never been to Spain. Most criollos were farmers or traders.

Then there were Africans, who were mostly slaves. They or their families had been kidnapped from different parts of Africa. Then they were forced to live in Cuba and work for the Spanish.

CUBAN AMERICANS

Finally, there were *mulattos*. Mulattos were people with mixed families. A mulatto person's mother could be African and his father Spanish. Or one of his parents could be criollo. There were a lot of different possibilities. Mulattos weren't very powerful either.

The First Cuban Migrations

Spain took over Cuba. It also took over parts of the Southern and Western United States. It used to own Florida. It also controlled parts of Texas, California, and other states.

People moved around throughout all the land Spain owned. If you lived in Cuba, you might travel to Florida at some point. It was easy since Spain owned both of them.

By the 1800s, Cubans were coming to the United States to go to college. They came to do business. They even came just to vacation.

On the other hand, Americans were visiting Cuba, too. They went on vacation, or they moved there and started up businesses.

Movement between Cuba and the United States has been happening for a long time. And it's still happening today.

Luis Rodríguez, Ladrones de Gallinas

chapter 3
Revolución!

Hatuey tried to start a **revolution** all the way back in the 1500s. He failed. But other Cubans would start other revolutions.

By the 1800s, many Cubans weren't happy with how things were run on the island. The Spanish controlled everything. No one else had any say.

Lots of Cubans wanted to be free from Spain. They wanted to make Cuba its own country. They didn't want it to be part of Spain any more.

This was true all over Latin America. People were rebelling against Spain. Mexico had already won independence. The United States had also just won its freedom from Britain. Cubans wanted their own revolution!

Not all Cubans agreed what was best. Some of them wanted complete freedom from Spain. Mulattos and African slaves wanted this. Other people wanted to stay part of Spain. Lots of criollos supported this. Finally, others wanted Cuba to become part of the United States.

Some people who wanted independence got in trouble. The government didn't like their views. So it exiled them. They forced them to leave the country.

Many of the exiles ended up in the United States. A lot of the time, they moved to New York City. In fact, New York City became a center for the Cuban **independence** movement.

> A **revolution** is when people try to get rid of the government and put a new government in its place.
>
> **Independence** means freedom. It means that the people of a land can run their own government.

Carlos Manuel de Céspedes

In New York, Cubans wrote about independence. They gave speeches on it. They created newspapers dedicated to it.

A lot of the people who wanted Cuban independence also didn't like slavery. They wanted to get rid of it. If they were going to be free from Spain, then shouldn't slaves be free too?

A lot of people joined the revolution after that. Many people didn't like slavery. So if a revolt meant that slavery would be over, they wanted to join.

The Ten Years War

The first battle in the Cuban revolution was in 1868. A man named Carlos Manuel de Céspedes was fed up with Spain. He got together an army and attacked the Spanish.

He was fairly successful. He had a lot of support, too. He even declared himself president. After awhile, he was thrown out, though. He couldn't keep up his success.

The revolution went on. New leaders took over. The connection between Cuba and the United States got stronger. Some Americans—both Cuban Americans and non-Cuban Americans—sent weapons and money to rebels. Also, more Cuban exiles moved to the United States.

And the revolution still went on. It lasted for ten long years. Finally, the rebels signed a **treaty** with Spain. The treaty ended the war. But it didn't win Cuba its freedom.

Some rebels didn't give up. They moved to other places, like the United States or other parts of Latin America. They spent a long time trying to get the revolution started again.

> A **treaty** is a written agreement between two countries.

General Maceo resisted the Spanish forces and kept alive Cuba's hopes for independence.

José Martí

Spain ended slavery in 1886. That meant that some of the rebels were happy. They got something they wanted. It seemed like Spain was pretty **secure** in Cuba for the moment.

Real Independence?

It didn't take long for another revolution to start. This time, it would be successful!

Spain used to own a lot of land the Americas. It owned most of South and Central America. It owned most of the Caribbean. By 1895, all it had left was Cuba and Puerto Rico, another island.

A man named José Martí would change that. Pretty soon, Spain wouldn't own Cuba either. Martí was an exile. He lived in New York City. He was a poet, a **journalist**, and a good speaker.

Statue of José Martí

Martí wanted Cubans to have total freedom. He didn't want Cuba to be part of Spain. He also didn't want Cuba to be part of the United States. Some people still did. They thought that Cuba should be another state in the United States.

Martí headed back to Cuba in 1895. He was killed in battle soon after that. But the revolution didn't stop. People were too excited, even though their leader had died.

Secure *means safe. It means that nothing is going to change, that things will stay steady.*

A **journalist** *is someone who writes news stories for newspapers and magazines.*

Revolución!

A poster for the for the Cuban revolution.

People kept fighting for three years. It was only Cubans who  fought. But Americans were getting interested.

The U.S. government kept a close eye on the revolution. There were American businesses in Cuba. Thousands of American citizens lived in Cuba. The United States wanted to protect these people and businesses.

The United States was also interested in making Cuba a state. It wanted Cuba for some of the same reasons that Spain had. Cuba had good land. It could make the United States a lot of money.

For a while, the United States didn't do any fighting in Cuba. They did send some battleships to wait off the coast. One day, one of the ships mysteriously exploded. We still don't know why. But Americans were sure that Spain had done it.

The United States went to war against Spain. Suddenly, the Cuban revolution changed names. It was now the Spanish-American War.

Four months later, the fighting was over. Spain surrendered. But not to Cuban rebels. It surrendered to the United States.

Now, instead of Spain as their ruler, Cubans had the United States. Cubans had wanted complete freedom. They were free from Spain now. But they were worried about becoming part of the United States.

The American military was in Cuba. The United States took part in making Cuba's new government. It took over Cuban trade. It seemed like the United States was taking over Cuba.

> "The Cuban problem needs, rather than a political solution, a social solution, and... the latter cannot be achieved except through mutual love, and forgiveness between the races."
>
> Letter from José Martí to Antonio Maceo, July 1882.

Sign found in Havana.

Luis Rodríguez, Llegada de mi Padre de Angola

chapter 4
New Leaders

Cuba went through a lot of changes in the twentieth century. Cubans hadn't seen the last of revolution, either. Some Cubans didn't like the change that was going on. They kept coming to the United States where things seemed calmer.

Bad Government

Things were getting pretty bad in Cuba by the 1930s. The government was especially bad. A man named Gerardo Machado was president. He was really a dictator. This means he had total control over the country. He used the army to get what he wanted. He also tortured and killed people who didn't agree with him.

People had had enough of him. They rebelled again. Machado was thrown out. The United States helped throw him out. Rebels and the United States helped another man into power. His name was Fulgencio Batista.

At first, Batista did some good things. He guaranteed a **minimum wage**. He created jobs for Cubans. It seemed like he would be good for the country.

It turned out that he wasn't so good. As time went on, he got worse and worse. He was a lot like Machado.

In 1944, Cubans voted against him. They didn't want him as president any more. He left Cuba and moved to Florida. But he wasn't done with Cuba.

> **Minimum wage** *is the lowest amount per hour that the government allows employers to pay their employees. If there is no minimum wage, than employers can pay their workers as little as they want.*

A few years later, he ran for president again. It didn't look like he would win. So he just overthrew the elected president. He declared himself Cuba's ruler.

Cuba got worse. Rich people got richer. But poor people got poorer. Crime happened more and more.

Batista used the military to punish people who disagreed with him. People were afraid to speak out against him. They might be tortured or murdered if they did.

Older Cubans still remember Batista's corruption.

Cubans were scared. Thousands of them left Cuba. They moved to the United States. But not many of them thought they were leaving forever. They wanted to come back once Batista was gone.

Fidel Castro

Most Americans have a bad impression of Fidel Castro. He's **communist**. Lots of Americans don't like communists. Lots of Cubans don't like Castro either. But there are other opinions about him too. Some people like him a lot.

Fidel Castro started out as a leader of a revolution. In the 1950s, Batista was still the dictator. There was a lot of crime. People were poor. Things were bad.

*A **communist** believes that the government should control all businesses rather than individuals. The money from businesses should be used then to help all the people in the country. Communism believes that no one should be very rich and no one should be very poor. It sounds like a good idea in some ways, but it hasn't always worked out very well.*

CUBAN AMERICANS

Fidel Castro was popular with ordinary people.

Cubans had a history of fighting back. This time was no different. A man named Fidel Castro started get people excited. He was a good speaker, like José Martí, another Cuban revolutionary had been.

Castro started putting together a small army. He and about a hundred other fighters attacked the army. They were fighting a thousand soldiers.

Castro lost that first battle. Several rebels were captured and either killed or put in prison. Castro was put in prison too.

Batista didn't feel very worried about Castro. There were only a hundred rebels after all. So he let Castro out of prison. That was a bad decision for Batista.

Castro attending a celebration with school children.

CUBAN AMERICANS

Once out of prison, Castro moved to Mexico. Lots of rebels followed him. He also traveled around the United States. Cubans in the United States supported him. They gave him money to buy supplies and weapons.

Non-Cubans helped Castro out too. The most famous is Che Guevara. He was a doctor from Argentina that fought for freedom all over Latin America.

Castro trained his rebels and made them into an army. They climbed mountains. They learned how to use weapons. They ran drills. They studied the writings of José Martí.

Pretty soon, Castro decided to go back to Cuba. He would bring his army with him. They boarded a boat headed to Cuba.

However, Batista knew they were coming. He had the army attack the rebels. Most of them were killed. Only twelve rebels ever made it to safety in the mountains.

Castro wasn't killed. His revolution seemed like it was going to fail, though. But he was determined. He regrouped. He got even more followers to add to his army.

The rebels started attacking the military again. They did it in secret and not in the open. People heard about the growing revolution. More and more people found the rebels. They joined the revolution.

Lots of **peasants** liked the rebels. The rebels let them use their hospital. They taught them to read. They told sugar plantations to pay more to the peasants who worked there—or else they would burn the plantations down.

In return, the peasants supported the rebels. They gave them food. They cleared roads for them.

Batista was tired of the rebels. He wanted to get rid of them. So he sent ten thousand soldiers to conquer them.

Peasants *are ordinary people who make their living from the land. They are usually poor and don't have much power.*

It didn't work. The rebels were very organized. And they had a lot of support. They outsmarted Batista's soldiers.

The army gave up. Castro's rebels took over. Batista even fled the country. The dictator was gone! But now what?

More Change

There were lots of Cubans in exile. They were waiting for Batista to leave Cuba. Now it had happened. Cubans came pouring back into the country.

Most people in Cuba were happy. Batista was gone. Changes for the better seemed to be happening. Castro and the rebels were good to poor people. Most people were poor, so they were going to do better now.

A few people weren't so happy. The Cubans who had supported Batista now fled. They were the ones in exile now.

But most Cubans were hopeful. Castro promised a better government. He promised a better more jobs and more money for everyone. He promised better education. There would be peace.

The rest of the world was worried, though. The United States government thought that Castro might be communist.

The basic idea of communism is to create a community where everyone is equal. All land and money is owned by everybody, not by individual people. Everyone helps out everybody else and gets help in return. It sounds like a good plan!

Communism has been tried in lots of countries. It usually doesn't work so well. No one is really equal. Dictators and bad governments take over. People end up worse off than they were before.

The U.S. government doesn't like communism. In the 1950s, people really hated communism. They were afraid that communists were going to take over more countries. So they were worried that Cuba would become communist.

Harvesting sugarcane in Cuba.

At first, Castro said he wasn't a communist. But he did a lot of things that said otherwise. He took big farms away from their owners. He gave them to the government. Then the government broke them up into smaller farms. They gave the small farms to poor people.

That made the poor people happy. But it made the original farm owners angry. They planned their own rebellions again Castro.

Soon, people began leaving Cuba again. Not everyone in Cuba liked that Castro and their country was becoming communist. A lot of rich people left. Business people left too. They were afraid that Castro would give their businesses to the government. They immigrated to the United States.

New Leaders

The United States and Cuba

Things got worse between the United States and Cuba. The United States didn't like that Cuba was communist. Americans wanted to put a stop to Castro's government.

The United States was the country that traded the most with Cuba. It bought almost all of the sugar grown in Cuba. But because the United States was angry, it threatened to stop trading with Cuba.

Castro didn't want that to happen. How would Cuba sell its sugar? So he made a deal with the Soviet Union instead. The Soviet Union was also communist. It was America's biggest **rival**. Castro would sell sugar to the Soviet Union.

> A **rival** is someone you compete with. You try to prove that you are better than that person, that you are stronger or smarter.

Havana

Cuba

Bay of Pigs

Map of Cuba, showing the Bay of Pigs.

Cubans living in the United States weren't happy either. They dropped anti-Castro pamphlets on Cuba. They even dropped bombs.

The United States finally stopped trading with Cuba. It also cut off all diplomatic relations. That means that the government of the United States refused to have anything to do with the government of Cuba. They wouldn't even talk to them.

In 1961, the United States actually sent the Army to Cuba. It invaded. Americans thought the invasion would trigger another revolution. Cubans would support the Army. Then they would get rid of Castro.

That didn't happen. Most of the people who had stayed in Cuba liked Castro. They didn't want to kick him out. They felt he had helped make their lives better. So Cubans fought back against the American Army. The Cubans attacked the invaders. And they won. The whole thing was called the Bay of Pigs Invasion.

After that, Cuba got closer to the Soviet Union. The Soviet Union liked that Cuba was so near to the United States. If the Soviet Union set up military bases on Cuba, it could easily attack the United States. The Soviet leader offered to build **nuclear missiles** on Cuba. Castro agreed.

> **Nuclear missiles** *are rockets that drop nuclear bombs.*

The United States found out. The Army prepared to invade Cuba again. This could have been a disaster. Now there were nuclear weapons involved. A nuclear war would have killed thousands or millions of people. People all over the world were scared.

Luckily, the leaders of the United States and the Soviet Union made a deal. Neither one really wanted a nuclear war. So the Soviet Union agreed to shut down the missiles.

No one asked Castro what he wanted. He was angry that they had decided without him. But a crisis had been avoided.

After that, Castro focused on running Cuba. Meanwhile, America turned its back on Cuba.

Luis Rodríguez, El Tres Viejo

42

chapter 5
Getting to America

Today, there are over a million Cubans in the United States. Many of them have been really successful. Of course, lots of different people are Cuban immigrants. Others haven't been so successful. There have been lots of things in the way of their success.

Some Cuban immigrants were welcomed with open arms into the United States. But others didn't have such a warm welcome. It all depended when they came to the United States.

The Golden Exiles

The Cubans who came to the United States in the 1950s and 1960s were welcomed warmly. They were fleeing Fidel Castro. A lot Americans didn't like Castro. So they liked anyone who didn't agree with him.

Sometimes, these Cuban immigrants are called the "Golden Exiles." That's because many of them were rich. They were educated. They were lawyers and doctors in Cuba. Some already spoke English well when they got here. They were people that Americans want in the United States.

Other immigrants from other countries are usually different. They want to leave their countries because there are no opportunities there. They have no jobs. They can't go to school. They can't go to the hospital. They don't have enough money. So they try their luck in the United States.

Sometimes these immigrants aren't as welcome in the United States. They don't speak English. They need more help to get used to their new country. So not all Americans want them in the United States.

Many of the people who from Cuba who had fled Castro had a lot to offer America. But getting used to living in the United States was still hard for them. They had to leave everything behind. They left their homes. They left their families. They left their friends.

There were things that helped them here. There was already a big Cuban population in the United States. The Cubans who had already made the move welcomed new immigrants. They helped them find jobs. They helped them learn English. They made them less homesick.

The United States government also helped the Golden Exiles out. It loaned them money. It helped them start their own businesses. It helped them get jobs.

Many of the Golden Exiles ended up living in Miami, Florida. Miami is very close to Cuba. Pretty soon, there were Cuban neighborhoods there. Today, some people call Miami "Little Havana." (Havana is the capital of Cuba.)

Cuban neighborhoods have lots of Cuban businesses. There are Cuban restaurants. The streets are named after Cuban things. You might even think you're actually in Cuba when you walk through them!

The Marielitos

Most of the exiles fleeing Castro came to the United States in the 1960s. In the 1970s, fewer Cubans came. Castro stopped letting people immigrate to the United States. The United States also stopped letting so many immigrants move in.

Then, in the 1980s, a flood of new Cubans came. Castro decided to let Cubans visit their families in America. Before, they hadn't been allowed to travel back and forth. So some people hadn't seen their friends and family for twenty years.

Lots of Cubans went. When they came back home, they brought back things from the United States. They brought back food. They brought back toasters. They brought back TVs. These were all things most Cubans didn't have.

A lot of Cubans suddenly wanted to go to the United States. They wanted to experience new things. They wanted to buy things. Life was often hard in Cuba. It seemed so much better in the United States!

Castro decided to let them go. Thousands of people traveled to Mariel, a city on the ocean. Meanwhile, Cubans in the United States heard what was happening. They sailed boats all the way to Cuba. There, they picked up Cubans who wanted to go to the United States. Then they took them back.

Some of the boats were sailed by honest people who wanted to help out Cubans. Others weren't. They were sailed by people who wanted money. They made Cubans pay a lot to get a ride in their boat.

A Cuban artist's painting of a young woman.

They stuffed people into small boats too. The boats were crowded. Some people even died because the boats were so crowded people couldn't breathe.

Americans weren't so happy that all these new Cubans were coming. They didn't welcome them like they had the Golden Exiles.

Newspapers and TV news called the new immigrants Marielitos. This was because they took boats from the city of Mariel. The news called the Marielitos criminals. It was true that a few were criminals. But most Marielitos were honest people. They just wanted to move out of Cuba.

Americans didn't want more Cubans for a lot of reasons. The Marielitos weren't doctors or lawyers. They were construction workers. They owned small businesses. They were ordinary people who did ordinary jobs.

The United States was having troubles of its own. Many Americans couldn't find jobs. They thought the Marielitos would take the jobs that there were. So Americans were angry.

Race was also an issue. A lot of Marielitos had dark skin. Americans saw them as black. At the time (and still today), **racism** was a big problem. Some Americans didn't want more black people coming to the United States.

> **Racism** *is the belief that people whose skin is a different color aren't as good and deserve to be treated unfairly.*

Some of the Marielitos immigrated illegally. They didn't have the right papers. They weren't supposed to come to the United States until they applied for permission. But they didn't have time. Applying to be an immigrant to the United States can take years. The Marielitos needed to leave right away. Maybe Castro wouldn't let them go in a month.

In the end, a million Marielitos came to America. Castro and the United States finally stopped the immigration. Castro was embarrassed that so many people hated living in Cuba. The United States was worried

Cuban Americans are an impportant part of the United States.

about having too many new immigrants.

Over the years, the Marielitos have proven that they're hardworking. They got jobs. They added something good to the United States.

The Raft People

In 1990, the Soviet Union collapsed. It fell apart. It didn't exist any more. Americans were happy. Their enemy had disappeared.

Things weren't so good for Cubans, though. The Soviet Union had helped them out. It traded with them. It bought Cuban sugar. Now Cubans didn't have that help.

Cubans Americans like these may face prejudice in the United States.

Hard times were ahead. Castro asked Cubans to make sacrifices. He asked them to stop doing things that cost a lot of money.

People in Cuba weren't happy. Things were hard before. Now they were even harder. So more people decided to leave.

This time, they had to leave on homemade rafts and boats. They didn't have fancy boats to take them across to Florida.

The United States is only 90 miles away from Cuba. But that's a long way for a homemade raft to sail. It's tiring to row all that way. And there are sharks. And storms. There isn't any fresh water. The sun gets very hot.

Despite the risks, people were willing to try it. They were called "raft people." Thousands of people tried to sail from Cuba to Florida.

A lot of times, the United States Coast Guard rescued people on rafts. But that meant that the people usually didn't reach the United States. The Coast Guard took them back to Cuba. Some of them made it to Florida, though.

These people were just one more group coming to the United States. Many groups of immigrants have left Cuba and moved to the United States over the years. Each group came for different reasons. But once they got to America, all of them started creating something new.

In the United States, they were Cuban Americans. They became part of the United States' mosaic.

Some Cubans were willing to risk death to go to Florida.

Luis Rodríguez, Noche Buena

chapter 6
Cuban American Culture Today

Imagine moving to a new country. Everything is different. Nobody knows where you came from.

Would you try to be the person you were before? Would you keep speaking English? Would you eat the food you used to like? Would you wear the same clothes? Or listen to the same music?

Or would you try to change and fit in? You would probably start to try to speak everybody else's language. Maybe you'd try new foods and listen to new music. You might start feeling like you have a new way of life.

In the end, you'd probably keep some of the old things you liked. And you would add some new things.

That's just what happens to many immigrants. They don't want to leave everything behind. They want to keep some of who they were. But they also want to fit into their new country. So they change some things about themselves.

It's no different for Cuban Americans. They have to figure out how to be American, but still be Cuban. It's not always very easy.

Family

Families are one way that Cuban Americans keep their Cuban identity. Cuban families are often really close. Grandparents, parents, aunts, uncles, sons, daughters, cousins—everybody lives together. Or lives close by. Or is visiting all the time.

Family is a very important part of Cuban culture.

Generations *are all the people who are born in a certain period. So your grandparents belong to one generation, your parents and your aunts and uncles to another, and you, your brothers and sisters, and your cousins to yet another.*

This happened all the time in Cuba. Many **generations** lived all together in one house. So when Cubans moved to the United States, they brought that tradition with them.

Of course, not all Cuban American families are like this. You can't say every Cuban American is any one thing. There are millions of Cuban Americans. They don't do everything exactly alike!

Cuban Americans whose families have been in the United States often don't fit this description. American families in general are less close. They don't all live together. Visits to grandparents are special occasions.

As Cubans have kids in the United States, those kids grow up in America. They become more American. One thing that happens is their families might stop being so close. Other Cuban Americans keep the family tradition alive.

Quinceañera

Cuban Americans have kept other Cuban **traditions** alive. The *quinceañera* is one.

Quinceañeras, or *quinces* for short, happen on girls' fifteenth birthdays. They mark when a girl stops being a kid and starts being more of an adult. It's kind of like a bar mitzvah (in the Jewish culture) or sweet-sixteen birthdays.

Girls dress up in fancy dresses. They have big parties. But first, the day starts with a church service. Only close friends and family go to this part. Then, more people arrive for dinner. Finally, the dancing starts. There is traditional dancing and also dancing to pop music.

Some quinces are small, while others are huge. Sometimes families spend a lot of money. They plan for them for weeks or months or even years.

A quinces is much more than an ordinary birthday party. It shows that a girl is growing up. People might treat her more as an adult after her quince. It's almost as big a day as her wedding day.

Religion

Religion was a big part of people's lives in Cuba. So it makes sense that it's important to a lot of Cuban Americans.

Most Cubans are Christian. A lot of them are Catholic. The very first Spanish explorers were Catholic. They brought their religion with them when

Traditions *are ways of doing things that have been handed down from grandparents to their children to THEIR children. They're the way things have been done for years and years.*

they came to the Cuba. They ended up **converting** a lot of Natives and African slaves to Catholicism.

Other Cubans are Protestants. Protestantism is another kind of Christianity. You are Protestant if you are Baptist. Or Methodist or Pentecostal. There are lots of different kinds of Protestants.

Most people in the United States are Protestant. As Cuba got closer to the United States over time, more Cubans became Protestants. Cubans also became Protestants when they moved to the United States.

Cuba has many different religions. Not everyone is Christian. Some follow a religion called Santería. Santería is actually a lot like Catholicism. There are saints. There is one God. But Santería is also different than Christianity. It comes from West African religions that slaves brought with them to Cuba a long time ago. Santeros (people who practice Santería) believe in spirits. These spirits are called Orishas. People pray to the spirits. The Orishas and the Catholic saints are all mixed together.

A few Cubans are Jewish. Most of them used to live in Europe. They were treated badly for being Jewish. So they moved away. Some moved to Cuba. Then, they moved again. Once Castro came to power in Cuba, Cuban Jews moved to the United States.

Art

Art is a big part of Cuban culture. It's a way for Cuban Americans to stay connected to Cuba. They can read a Cuban novel. Or they can look at a Cuban painting.

There are lots of Cuban writers. José Martí, the revolutionary, is probably the first really famous one. He wrote to **inspire** other Cubans to revolt against Spain.

Newer Cuban and Cuban American writers still write about freedom. They write about being exiled.

Some Cuban American writers have even won Pulitzer Prizes. Pulitzers are big awards for writers. Oscar Hijuelos and Nilo Cruz have both won them. Other famous Cuban American writers include Christina Garcia and Achy Obejas.

Some Cuban American artists are painters. Painting lets them explore their culture and their experiences. Cubans create all sorts of paintings. Some are **murals** on the walls of city buildings. Some hang in fancy museums.

Finally, music is a type of art found all over Cuba and in the Cuban American community. There is classical Cuban music. There is salsa music. There is popular dance music.

Salsa is a form of Cuban music that's like no other. It comes from a mix of African music, jazz, and rock and roll. It started in Cuba but has spread farther than that. Cuban Americans helped bring it to the United States.

Murals *are huge paintings that are often painted on an entire wall of a building.*

Cuban art depicting Eleggua, an ancient native chief.

Luis Rodriguez, El Entierro

chapter 7
Famous Cuban Americans

You've already seen what Cuban Americans add to the United States. A few Cuban Americans have done so much that today they're famous.

Desi Arnaz

Have you ever heard of the TV show *I Love Lucy*? It's one of the most successful TV shows in American history. And it starred a Cuban American!

I Love Lucy was a comedy about a woman and her family and friends. The woman was played by Lucille Ball, a popular actress. She was married to a man named Desi Arnaz.

Arnaz was born in Cuba. He moved to the United States when he was a kid. He later became a musician. He played the Cuban drums and sang Cuban songs.

Ball agreed to act in *I Love Lucy*. But only if Arnaz played her husband. At first, the show's creators didn't want to let him. They wanted to show an "American" family. That didn't include a Cuban American husband.

They gave in. Arnaz played Ricky Ricardo, a Cuban singer. It turned out

Desi Arnaz

they made the right decision. Audiences loved the show. *I Love Lucy* was super successful.

Arnaz was one of the first Cubans to become famous in the United States. He sometimes spoke Spanish on air. He talked about Cuba once in a while. He played Cuban music. For some Americans, it was the first time they had ever seen a Cuban person.

Celia Cruz

Celia Cruz is one the biggest salsa music stars ever. She even helped to create salsa music.

Cruz was born in the 1920s in Havana, Cuba. She had a big family. She was poor growing up. But she was good at singing.

She couldn't afford to take lessons. She found other ways of singing, though. She sang in contests all around Cuba. Sometimes she won.

Eventually, she sang with a band called La Sonora Matancera. They released a record. The record was a huge success. People listened to it all over Latin America and in the United States. Everybody in Cuba was listening to the band.

In 1960, Cruz and her band moved to the United States. She didn't do so well at first. Then, she started singing salsa.

Cruz became famous. She was a great singer. She also had a one-of-a-kind style. She wore flashy, colorful clothes. She got audiences excited. No one was quite like Celia!

She never lost her fame. She kept putting out successful records. By the time she died in 2003, she had made more than fifty albums.

Roberto C. Goizueta

You've probably never heard the name Roberto C. Goizueta before. But you have probably drank Coca-Cola.

Celia Cruz

Goizueta was born in Cuba in 1931. His father was rich. He was a sugar producer. Because his family was so rich, he could go to college at Yale University in the United States.

Then he decided to start his own business. He started working for Coca-Cola in Havana. At first, things were going well for Goizueta. He had a good job. He was married and had three kids. But then Castro came to power. Castro didn't like the American companies that were in Cuba. Including Coca-Cola.

So Goizueta and his family moved to the United States. Once there, he kept on working for Coca-Cola. He kept getting promotions. Pretty soon, he was one of the most powerful people—Cuban or not—in the business world. He ran the whole company.

It wasn't easy being Cuban at the top. People thought of Coca-Cola as an American company. How could a Cuban run it?

But Goizueta was a great businessman and people stopped complaining. Coca-Cola became an even bigger company while Goizueta was in charge.

Famous Cuban Americans

Cuba as a Spark

Cuba is still an important issue in the United States. Cuba has always been something that Americans have argued about. They still do.

Right now, Cuba and the United States don't have a good relationship. They don't trade with each other. Americans aren't allowed to go to Cuba. Cubans aren't allowed to go to the United States.

That makes Cuban Americans' lives hard. They want to be Cuban. And they want to be American. It's hard when the two countries don't get along.

Eventually things will change. Fidel Castro is very old. He's actually given up power to his brother. Raul Castro now rules Cuba. Raul is old too. Who will take over next?

Pretty soon a new government will take over. Maybe the new government will be communist. Maybe it won't.

But no matter what, a new government might makes things better between Cuba and the United States. And things will change.

Will Cuban Americans move to Cuba? Will more Cubans move to the United States? How will Cuba be different?

There are a lot of questions. However, it's safe to say that most Cuban Americans are here to stay. Many feel like the United States is home. They have helped make America a stronger, more interesting place to live. We wouldn't want to lose them!

Time Line

1492	Christopher Columbus claims Cuba for Spain.
1526	The Spanish bring African slaves to Cuba for the first time.
1868–78	Ten Year War of independence ends with Spain still in control.
1886	Slavery on Cuba ends.
1895	Jose Marti leads a second war of independence.
1898	The United States wins the Spanish American War and gains Cuba.
1902	Cuba becomes independent.
1954	Batista takes over Cuba.
1959	Castro overthrows Batista and takes control of Cuba.
1961	America breaks off all diplomatic relations with Cuba. The tries to attack Cuba at the Bay of Pigs, but the mission fails. Castro sides with the Soviet Union.
1962	The Cuban Missile Crisis ends with the Soviet Union promising to remove all missiles from Cuba.
1980	Castro allows Cubans to leave from the port of Marielo.
1990	The Soviet Union collapses.
2008	Raul Castro takes over as president, days after Fidel announces his retirement.
2011	Cuba passes law allowing individuals to buy and sell private property for first time in 50 years.

Find Out More

IN BOOKS

Ancona, George. *Cuban Kids*. Tarrytown, N.Y.: Marshall Cavendish, 2000.

Cannarella, Deborah. *Cuban Americans.* North Mankato, Minn.: Child's World, 2003.

Roque, Ismael. *Cuba for Kids.* London, UK: Cuba for Kids Foundation, 2000.

ON THE INTERNET

Cuban Cultural Center
www.cubanculturalcenter.org

Cuban Culture
www.cuban-culture.com

The Cuban Experience
library.thinkquest.org/18355/culture.html

The History of Cuba
historyofcuba.com/cuba.htm

Index

Picture Credits

About the Author and the Consultant

Frank DePietro is an editor and author who lives in Upstate New York. He studied anthropology in college, and he continues to be fascinated with the world's cultures, art, and folklore.

Dr. José E. Limón is professor of Mexican-American Studies at the University of Texas at Austin where he has taught for twenty-five years. He has authored over forty articles and three books on Latino cultural studies and history. He lectures widely to academic audiences, civic groups, and K–12 educators.